Whether y
you are think
know one tru
challenging a
you considered it your ministry? Tamara Chilver is a
homeschooling mom of five. She's heard it all from
supporters and critics alike. Her view is splendidly
simple— Christ leads her *and* her homeschool.
Maybe you haven't considered what you're
accomplishing with your child a calling, but it is
indeed! It's God's calling for your life at this stage.

Through wisdom from God and life experience,
Tamara tackles one false statement at a time- ones
said to us and ones we've thought to ourselves. She
is a one woman cheerleading squad! Each chapter in
Grace for the Homeschool Mom is punctuated with
Scriptures pointing to God as our Divine Teacher
and how homeschooling fits into God's plan for
our children. She is transparently honest and never
implies that she's had an easy road. As we read of
her struggles and even devastating circumstances,
we come to the realization that we aren't alone and
don't have to be perfect.

Every mom (homeschooler or not) needs to hear
this and hear it often. No doubt there will be days
when you need a spiritual uplifting, and this book
should remain at arm's length at all times.
~Liz Terek

Grace for the Homeschool Mom is the book to grab when you need encouragement. The way Tamara Chilver divides the book is a real time saver for busy moms. Just pull the book off your shelf, scan the table of contents for the struggle you are facing, and read the encouraging chapter. The chapters are short but powerful. Tamara keeps it real by sharing her struggles and how she depends on God to overcome them. Thanks to Tamara for another great book!
~Jerilyn Lyons

Grace for the Homeschool Mom is a valuable treasure! This book identifies a plethora of myths and lies that homeschool families battle regularly. The truth of God's grace behind each myth and lie, is not only revealed, but is supported with applicable Scriptures. This book challenged me to confront the lies that have torn at me for years and also deal with those that I "thought" I had resolved on my own. I am now ready to engage in year six of homeschooling with a happy and obedient heart, not to be distracted by fabrications anymore.
~MJ Harris

When I first felt a tug at my heart to teach my daughter at home, I knew I needed to take it to the Lord. Before even considering curriculum, I prayed and was led to *Grace for the Homeschool Mom*. It was inspiring and encouraging! It was as if someone else who had already walked this path knew all my doubts and insecurities and had the Biblical answers right there waiting. I know the path ahead may not be easy, but I know I don't walk it alone. Thank you Tamara!
~Dee Domingo

GRACE

for the Homeschool Mom

Tamara L. Chilver

TLC Editions
Fort Myers, Florida

GRACE
for the Homeschool Mom

Information on Tamara L. Chilver's resources
can be found on-line at www.teachingwithtlc.com.

While the author has made every effort to provide
accurate Internet addresses at the time of
publication, the author is not responsible for errors
or changes that occur after publication.

ISBN: 978-1492352860
Published by TLC Editions
Fort Myers, FL

A special thanks to:
Leslie Simpson- cover design
Haleigh Katwaroo- editing

Dedication

If I could use one word to describe my spiritual journey for the past seven years, it would be *grace*. During this time, I have been incredibly blessed to have a close circle of friends who prayed fervently for me, cried with me, encouraged me, and praised God with me. I can't imagine what this journey would have been like without their persistent prayers and constant support. They believed in me when I was filled with questions and doubt. They stood on the sidelines cheering me on during my race when all I wanted to do is quit. They kept me focused on God's Word to regain the strength to keep moving forward.

Thank you Candis Daugherty, Traci Edwards, MJ Harris, Robin Hayes, Haleigh Katwaroo, Jerilyn Lyons, Christi McGinnis, Robin Mitchell, Marie Mosley, Chris Perkins, Priscilla Wolfe, and Karen Zeigler for being such faithful prayer warriors and reminding me that His grace is always more than enough.

I pray that every homeschool mom who reads this book will be blessed by these lessons in grace that God has taught me. They have transformed me as a wife, mother, and home educator. Now the time has come for moms to take a deep breath, embrace His amazing grace, and fall deeper in love with Him.

Acts 20:24- "I consider my life worth nothing to me; my only aim is to finish the race and complete the task the Lord Jesus has given me— the task of testifying to the good news of God's grace."

Table of Contents

Introduction

Goodbye worry, fear, doubt, and guilt. Hello grace.

Have you ever spoken to a veteran homeschool mom who has taught a child all the way through graduation from high school? There is just something different about those moms. They seem so relaxed while schooling their other children, while remaining firm and steadfast in their faith. We look at them with awe and wonder. They are the admirable heroes of homeschooling. They have fought the enemy's lies in battle and had the strength and courage to continue the course. What's their secret? Most will tell you it is God's amazing grace.

God's unlimited grace is working to set you free. Free from worry, fear, doubt, and guilt. He knows you have struggled with desperate issues. He knows this path is difficult, but His grace is reaching out to you to deliver you. His grace can make you feel renewed, refreshed, and restored. The means to your victory in homeschoooling with peace is through accepting His grace.

Grace for the Homeschool Mom addresses the most common lies, fears, temptations, traps, and pitfalls that homeschool moms face. Use this book as a reference to arm yourself with God's grace and His Word to rebuke the deceptions of the enemy. Break away from the enemy's bondage and begin to experience freedom in your homeschool journey the way God intended.

Chapter 1
The Secret Weapon— God's Amazing Grace

Homeschool moms tend to carry a lot of extra burdens around with them compared to other moms. We are fully aware that we are going against the norm, which makes us easy targets for the enemy's deceptions. But here is the secret to lightening our load, God's amazing grace.

Grace is God's unmerited favor. Grace is God's promise to do for us what we cannot do for ourselves. It accomplishes what is otherwise impossible for us to accomplish. It is what frees us to enjoy the homeschool journey. God loves you and is proud of you for choosing the more difficult path. He will bless you abundantly for your obedience.

God's Word: Ephesians 2:8-9- "For it is by grace you have been saved, through faith— and this is not from yourselves, it is the gift of God— not by works, so that no one can boast."

In this verse, we learn that God's grace is a gift. No matter how hard we work, it cannot be earned.

God's Word: Ephesians 4:1-4- "I urge you to live a life worthy of the calling you have received. Be completely humble and gentle; be patient, bearing with one another in love. Make every effort to keep the unity of the Spirit through the bond of peace. There is one body and one Spirit, just as you were called to one hope when you were called."

Doesn't this vividly paint a picture of what homeschooling is really about? It is a calling that requires us to be humble, gentle, patient, and filled with love for our children and husband. We're also told to make every effort to keep peace and unity. For wives and mothers, this begins at home. The last verse reminds us of how we are called. God's Word is so beautiful and encouraging.

Did you know that Paul speaks of grace in two ways? The first is how people are saved by grace. The second is how God's grace also provides special gifts or abilities for your ministry, which can include teaching. Your family is your most important ministry, and God has given you the gift of teaching to equip you for your calling. It reaffirms that God doesn't always call the equipped, but He equips the called.

Chapter 2
The Hidden Agenda

Before we can address the worries, fears, doubts, and guilt that can make us second-guess our calling to homeschool, we must first realize their source. The enemy will do anything he can to stop you from fulfilling your calling. I have been homeschooling for 15 years and have seen the exact same tactics used against me and others over and over again. I'm tired of falling for these lies and have been a victim for far too long. I am refusing to believe them ever again. They are simply not true!

I am deeply saddened to see my friends and other home educators struggle with the same deceptions. My heart breaks when homeschool moms leave God's path because these lies have weighed them down for too long. They are weary and tired and have met depression face-to-face. They are my inspiration for this book. Tears are streaming down my cheeks as I type because I've seen this happen too many times. I do not want one more mother to fall victim to the enemy. I wish I could hug all the mothers who are at the place of indecision and say, "You are doing a fabulous job. God knows your heart. He knows your family even better than you do.

He knows your specific calling, which is unique and created only for you. He knows you are doing your best. Keep calm and homeschool on!"

Why does the enemy even bother with a mom at home with her children? Our job may seem monotonous, and some days even meaningless, but the reality is we are raising up an army for God. The enemy opposes us most when we are doing the call of God.

I was recently sharing with my homeschool friends how I was working on this book. I made the comment to them that I was amazed after talking to hundreds of moms about the enemy's lies, that he chooses to use the exact same ones repeatedly. Even word for word. I made the remark that I wondered why he didn't get more creative with his lies. Their unified response was, "Because they work! Why change them if we continue to believe them?"

It's time that homeschool moms come together in learning how to recognize the enemy's common tactics. No longer will we be the victim of these blatant attacks from the enemy. We are overcomers in Christ and will only believe God's Truth from this day on. We are uniting and continuing this journey together.

How can you protect yourself? First, you must acknowledge the enemy exists and become aware of his attacks, which include lies and temptations. Next, stand firm against the attacks in Jesus Christ. Declare the Truths in scripture until the opposition is gone.

The Truth: There is no need for believers to fear their spiritual enemy. While the enemy has the freedom to tempt and harass Christians, he has no direct authority over us. Jesus is our Defender. His Word is our sword and His armor provides us with the protection we need against the enemy's attacks. Don't be afraid to tell the enemy to get lost!

God's Word: Matthew 16:23- "Get behind me, Satan! You are a stumbling block to me; you do not have in mind the concerns of God, but merely human concerns."

James 4:6-7- "But he gives us more grace. That is why Scripture says: 'God opposes the proud but shows favor to the humble.' Submit yourselves, then, to God. Resist the devil, and he will flee from you."

Ephesians 6:10-18- "Finally, be strong in the Lord and in his mighty power. Put on the full armor of God, so that you can take your stand against the devil's schemes. For our struggle is not against flesh and blood, but against the rulers, against the authorities, against the powers of this dark world and against the spiritual forces of evil in the heavenly realms. Therefore put on the full armor of God, so that when the day of evil comes, you may be able to stand your ground, and after you have done everything, to stand. Stand firm then, with the belt of Truth buckled around your waist, with the breastplate of righteousness in place, and with your feet fitted with the readiness that comes from the gospel of peace. In addition to all of this, take up the shield of faith, with which you can extinguish all the flaming arrows of the evil one. Take the helmet of salvation and the sword of the Spirit, which is the word of God."

Chapter 3

Beware of the stumbling blocks.

As we begin our walk with grace tightly tucked away in our backpacks, I need to warn you that the homeschooling path is a bumpy trail. Since it is a road less traveled, it tends to have more stumbling blocks along the way. However, once we learn how to recognize them, we can use God's Word to step over these stumbling blocks, or simply pick them up and toss them aside instead of tripping on them.

Let's first talk about the comments from the not-so-supportive world we live in, so we can avoid being tempted to start running the other direction. These comments can be from friends, family members, or strangers and can rob you of your confidence and joy. When people say these comments to you, they are simply stating their own doubts and questions on how they would handle your situation. Some days these comments never make us blink, but on those "other days" where we may be at our wits' end, these comments can make us second guess our decision to homeschool. Sometimes we think, "Hmmm. Maybe they have a point, and I have made the wrong decision."

The Truth: No, you haven't. Be confident in your calling and the decisions you have made. Stand firm and trust God would never lead you down the wrong path.

God's Word: Hebrews 10:35-36- "So do not throw away your confidence; it will be richly rewarded. You need to persevere so that when you have done the will of God, you will receive what he has promised."

Proverbs 3: 5-6- helps us to remember to keep trusting our Creator and the path He has for us. "Trust in the Lord with all your heart and lean not on your own understanding; in all your ways submit to him, and he will make your paths straight."

Notice we have to submit to Him and completely trust Him. We can't trust what we see or feel, only trust Him. Let's now go over some of the comments you may have heard from others.

I could never homeschool.

Following God's plan is not always easy. To be quite honest, it is a sacrifice. Let's revisit the days you had to die to yourself. Recall the first year of your child's life. Remember how your world revolved around your little one's schedule, including: when you took a shower, when you ate, when you slept, and what time you ran errands. Remember how you chose to not complain but rather to joyfully savor the high calling of motherhood.

When we homeschool, we make the same sacrificial decision to die to ourselves again. We work, play, eat, and sleep around our children's homeschool schedule. We can choose to complain about the lack of "mom-time" or choose to enjoy the time together as a family.

When others say to you, "Oh, I could never homeschool." what they really mean is, "I don't want to do that. I would have to sacrifice my personal time." or "You are so brave. I respect you. I am too scared to attempt that."

The next time someone says to you, "I could never homeschool." just humbly ask, "Why not?"

The Truth: Any mother God calls to homeschool is more than capable for the job.

God's Word: Matthew 16:24- Then Jesus said to his disciples, "Whoever wants to be my disciple must deny themselves and take up their cross and follow me."

You must have a lot of patience.

I was not born with such a super-sized amount of patience that I thought I would keep on having more children until all my patience was finally used up. Nope. It did not happen that way. I just learned patience along my parenting journey. The more children I had, the more lessons I had in patience. The same is true about homeschooling. I have learned to have more patience because of homeschooling.

We need patience so God can mold us into His likeness. We should acknowledge our trials as part of God's plan, and welcome them with patience and hope. Even though I love my children in an indescribable way, there are still days that I lack the patience for this calling. The older I get, the more I realize how much I need God's grace. I long for His mercy. I need His forgiveness. I am nothing without Him.

The Truth: Being a mother will always require patience, even if your children are not with you all day. We all have areas we are weak in because we are all imperfect. God knows that. He is working on us. All He asks is for us to continue to follow His leading and to persevere.

God's Word: James 1:2-4- "Count it all joy when you fall into various trials, knowing that the testing of your faith produces patience. But let patience have its perfect work, that you may be perfect and complete, lacking nothing."

1 Corinthians 13:4-8 is a wonderful description of how we should love our family. "Love is patient, love is kind. It does not envy, it does not boast, it is not proud. It does not dishonor others, it is not self-seeking, it is not easily angered, it keeps no record of wrongs. Love does not delight in evil but rejoices with the truth. It always protects, always trusts, always hopes, always perseveres. Love never fails."

My kids would drive me crazy!

That is exactly what a close friend of mine told me years ago. She jokingly said her favorite part of the day was putting her kids on the school bus every morning. The ironic part is a few months later that same friend was planning to homeschool and even began a homeschool group at my church. God not only changed her heart in a few short months, but He used her to lead many other home educators. How awesome is that!

As far as my children driving me crazy, there are some days they do. But I've noticed this usually happens when I am distracted and not homeschooling like I should be. For instance, I occasionally make a "quick" stop at my desk during a busy time of the day. My children are waiting for my next instruction and then start goofing around. I become frustrated because I am trying to concentrate and wrap up an email, which usually leads to anger. This happened because I was not doing what I should have been. When I am focused, my children tend to stay focused.

I treasure my time at home with my five children and feel so blessed to be their mother. As I've already seen one child of mine grow into an adult, I know that the days may go by slow but the years go by fast.

The Truth: All parents feel like their children drive them crazy at some point, no matter if they attend school or not. From homework wars to last-minute school projects, parents who have their children attending school will still have days they want to pull their hair out. This is normal. It's all part of parenting. Cling to God. Ask for His help. You are not alone in this journey. He is walking right by your side.

God's Word: Exodus 18:18- "You and these people who come to you will only wear yourselves out. The work is too heavy for you; you cannot handle it alone."

I am just not a homeschool mom.

My best friend of 36 years, who happens to be a

former public school teacher, was visiting me at a homeschool convention a few months ago. Even though her oldest daughter wants to be homeschooled, my friend whispered to me, "I am just not a homeschool mom."

I said, "Look around. Almost every mom here at the convention has said that. You are not alone."

I don't feel any different as a homeschool mom than a regular mom. I don't wear denim jumpers. I don't sew all my children matching outfits. I don't grind my own wheat or bake my own bread. I'm just an average mom who wears flip-flops and my hair in a ponytail, and I ask for God's grace every day to complete whatever He wants me to do.

The Truth: Homeschool moms are regular moms that God has called to educate their children at home. What makes them stand apart from other mothers is their submission and commitment to God's sovereign plan for their family.

God's Word: Jeremiah 29:11- " 'For I know the plans I have for you,' declares the Lord, 'plans to prosper you and not to harm you, plans to give you hope and a future.' "

I don't know how you do it all.

Every mom has a lot on her plate, regardless of if she homeschools or not. I have learned some time-saving tricks over the years that I discuss in *Simplify Your Homeschool Day*, but I don't do it *all*. My laundry is piled up. There are some nights we eat cereal or grilled cheese sandwiches for dinner. I am years behind in scrap-booking. I wish I had more time to exercise than I do. And I always feel like I could be doing more in homeschooling. But I remind myself that scripture says, "In all you do, do it unto the Lord." Never does it say to do it all.

The Truth: Doing it all is a misconception the enemy wants mothers to believe. Even if your child attended school, you still wouldn't have time to do it all. Learn how to fully embrace the beauty of each season of your life. It is a gift from God.

God's Word: Colossians 3:23-24-"Whatever you do, work at it with all your heart, as working for the Lord, not for human masters, since you know that you will receive an inheritance from the Lord as a reward. It is the Lord Christ you are serving."

I encourage you to read Ecclesiastes 3. Here are some key verses that help us appreciate every season we experience.

Ecclesiastes 3:1- "There is a time for everything, and a season for every activity under the heavens."

Ecclesiastes 3:11- "He has made everything beautiful in its time."

Ecclesiastes 3:12-13 "I know that there is nothing better for people than to be happy and to do good while they live. That each of them may eat and drink, and find satisfaction in all their toil—this is the gift of God."

I don't have the courage you do.

Homeschooling is growing seven times faster than the rate of public school enrollment. I witnessed this explosive growth at this year's Florida Parent Educators Association (FPEA) convention that had thousands of parents beginning their journeys. I was also very surprised to see my E-book, *On the Fence About Homeschooling?*, quickly become a homeschool best-seller. So why are moms all of a sudden having the courage to homeschool?

It could be that parents are viewing the powerful and convicting movie, *IndoctriNation*, since churches across the United States are sharing this video with their congregations. It could be that parents are beginning to see the enemy's deceptions and realizing that whatever God calls them to, He will equip them along the way. It could be that parents feel more confident with the plethora of high-quality resources and teaching tools available.

The Truth: God commands us to be strong and courageous. You were created to be the leader for your child. Let him see you follow Jesus. No one will protect your child like you will. No one will love your child like you do. It makes absolute sense when God calls you to educate your child. You are the perfect person for the position!

God's Word: Deuteronomy 31:6- "Be strong and courageous. Do not be afraid or terrified because of them, for the Lord your God goes with you; he will never leave you nor forsake you."

2 Timothy 2:1- "Be strong in the grace that is in Christ Jesus."

I don't have the time to homeschool like you do.

We all have the same amount of time per day, and we will make time for things that are most important to us. Many mothers do not feel called to homeschool because they never ask for God's guidance in the area of education for their children. We pray for job changes and where to buy a house but often overlook the education options.

It could be due to our society teaching there is only one way to pursue an education. When I majored in education, not one professor mentioned the option of homeschooling. Compounding the problem, most of our parents had only one option of education with the lack of availability of private schools and homeschooling was unheard of in their time. Therefore, many of our older mentors never suggested we homeschool or encouraged the option of homeschooling with us as it was foreign to them.

Most homeschool moms will be quick to acknowledge that homeschooling was not their original plan for their child's education. God revealed His plan to them and they chose to follow Him.

The Truth: Homeschooling may not be God's will for every family, but we still need to seek His wisdom and gain a clear understanding of His purpose in this area of our lives and adjust our plans accordingly.

Proverbs 19:21- "Many are the plans in a person's heart, but it is the Lord's purpose that prevails."

Psalm 90:12- "Teach us to number our days, that we may gain a heart of wisdom."

Aren't you worried your child may not be socialized?

Socialization is defined as knowing how to act appropriately in various situations. Children in public schools are provided with minimal opportunities to socialize in a real-world sense. In a school setting, children are segregated by age and ability. The children socialize primarily with other people who are the same age and perform at the same ability. As adults, our social interactions are rarely this way. Think about the last time you were in a room filled with adults your exact age. It just doesn't happen in real life.

Several decades ago, there was ample time to socialize at school during unstructured activities. Schools are quite different today. When I taught in a public school, I was surprised at the lack of time that children were given to socialize. Assigned seating in the school cafeteria meant children were no longer allowed to choose who they would like to sit with and talk to. Recess did not exist at some schools due to safety concerns, and most physical education was structured activities, which allowed little time for socialization. There were also fewer cooperative learning activities since more time was spent preparing for standardized tests.

Homeschooled children tend to have friends of all ages because many participate in homeschool and church groups with children of various ages. Since home educated children can complete their schoolwork much quicker than their peers in a traditional school setting, and they have no homework, the time afforded to socialize is far greater. Many days my children are outside playing while their neighborhood friends are still completing homework.

The Truth: Other children are inside four walls all day while your child has been to the grocery store, the bank, and the park. Remember, the definition of socialization is to know how to act appropriately in *various* situations.

God's Word: Romans 12:2- "Do not conform to the pattern of this world, but be transformed by the renewing of your mind. Then you will be able to test and approve what God's will is—his good, pleasing and perfect will."

You're the worst example of a homeschool mom.

Most people will not verbally say this to you, but every now and then you might get the impression this is what they are thinking, especially when it is accompanied by eye rolling and head shaking. It occasionally goes along with other thoughts, such as: "Do you see how your child acts in public? Don't you remember what grades you received when you were in high school? How could you possibly educate your child effectively?"

I admit that I have spent less time disciplining my younger children compared to my older children. Even though I have learned to choose my battles wisely, we still have family rules and consequences. However, my children's behavior can shift immediately with no warning.

For example, my children were complimented by a couple who was eating dinner next to us last week at a restaurant. They said they never even heard my children and were so impressed with their fantastic behavior. Fast forward to the next afternoon when we were at a rather large children's museum and my ten-year-old, who was standing two feet away from me, decided to pull the fire alarm (later to learn he did it to see if those really worked). What? My jaw hit the floor and my eyes popped out of my head. I was speechless. My son began to cry after he realized what a commotion he had caused. It felt like an eternity standing there waiting for someone to find the special key to turn it off while people scurried about.

The Truth: We all are a work in progress. None of us are perfect. We will make mistakes no matter how hard we try not to and so will our children. The great news is God already knew every detail about you and your child when He called you to homeschool. Be confident in your calling. He is working on you and through you.

God's Word: Matthew 5:11-12- "Blessed are you when people insult you, persecute you and falsely say all kinds of evil against you because of me. Rejoice and be glad, because great is your reward in heaven."

Philippians 1:6- "Being confident of this, that he who began a good work in you will carry it on to completion until the day of Christ Jesus."

He would never call me.
That is more than I can handle.

This statement concerns me more than the others. I have seen the pattern repeat itself too many times. A mother believes God would never call her to homeschool. She begins to pray about it, and then God gently points her to homeschooling. She knows in her heart what God wants her to do, but she begins to list reasons to justify why it cannot possibly happen (many of which are in this book). Sadly, most will choose a different path and miss out on God's blessings.

When I was a teenager, my aunt shared a tragic story that has stayed with me. It is about my aunt's close friend who was in a horrible car accident. In a second, her life was forever changed when a car hit her and her family head-on. She looked aside and saw her husband in the driver's seat and instantly knew in her heart he did not survive.

Then she called out to her two children sitting in the backseat. Neither one responded. Through her pain, she tried her best to wiggle through the debris that she was trapped in to try to touch her children since she was unable to turn around. When she finally was able to touch them, she could tell by their lifeless little hands they both had passed away.

In that moment, she became a widow. She would no longer be referred to as a wife nor would she hear the word "mom" ever again from her two precious children.

I just can't imagine the depth of grief she experienced. Her role as a mother and wife was instantly taken away. The people she loved the most were gone. This story is the reason why the common statement, "God never gives you more than you can handle" really bothers me. My aunt's friend had MUCH more than she could handle.

A few years ago, I was going through a hard trial, even though it was not nearly as difficult as my aunt's friend. But this particular trial tested and stretched my faith like no other in my past. Throughout it, several people would make the comment to me, "God never gives you more than you can handle."

All that did was make me feel worse and like a failure. It made me feel like I was supposed to be better and stronger than I was. Other times, that statement made me angry at God and I thought, "Why would God allow all of this to happen to me? How strong does He think I am?"

And then my angel of a friend instantly strengthened my faith. She said to me, "God does allow more than you can handle, but He helps you handle what you are given."

That was powerful! Yes, sometimes God allows more than I feel like I can handle but He promised never to leave me or forsake me, so I know that means He will help me handle whatever He allows. What a release! No more guilt that I wasn't strong enough. God wanted me on my knees so I would lean on Him and depend solely on His strength to help me through the fire, valley, wilderness, desert, or whatever else you'd like to call it.

If you have a child that requires much more attention and patience than the average child and you think parenting is more than you can handle, you are definitely correct. If you are questioning how you can do it all as a mom, wife, and educator and you feel it is more than you can handle, you are certainly right. If you find homeschooling is extremely challenging and leaves you exhausted and depleted, and you feel it is more than you can handle, you are absolutely correct.

Does that mean God wants you to stop homeschooling? No, it does not. It means that God will help you do it if you trust and lean on Him for guidance and strength. We need to continually stay focused on Him. Magnify Him and not the difficulty of your circumstances. Remember if God calls you to it, He will see you through it.

The Truth: God likes to show us that through Him all things are possible. He often takes the area we are weakest in to use us in mighty ways. That is how He gets the glory. All eyes must remain on Him to complete the task.

God's Word: Matthew 19:26- "With man this is impossible, but with God all things are possible."

Dealing with Unsupportive Comments

As we close this chapter and begin to walk in a new direction, I encourage you keep focused on your calling even when others are not supportive.

God's Word: Deuteronomy 5:32- "So be careful to do what the Lord your God has commanded you; do not turn aside to the right or to the left."

Galatians 5:7 clearly shows how just one person can slow us down or even stop us altogether from following God's path. It says, "You were running a good race. Who cut in on you to keep you from obeying the Truth?"

Fill your heart with God's Word, rejoice that you have the opportunity to be with your children, and keep on moving forward. God promises He will reward your faithfulness.

Beware of the stumbling blocks.

Chapter 4
Dodge the arrows.

Sometimes the spiritual battle of the mind can be extremely intense. I know from past experiences how it can weigh you down until you are on your knees begging for mercy. The enemy knows your deepest insecurities and will use those as his ammunition. Realize you have a choice. You can choose to believe the lies, or you can choose to ignore them and cling to God's Truth.

We have to stand firm and defend ourselves. If someone was to tell you a bold lie about your child, your mommy instinct would come out full force to defend your child. We have to do the same when the enemy tells us these deceptions. It is up to us to defend our families. Let's choose the path of Truth.

Now I need you to put on your shield of faith for this part of our walk together, so we can extinguish all the flaming arrows the evil one will throw our way.

I am not qualified to teach my child.

Usually this lie is later followed by, "Who am I kidding? I really thought I would be able to do this."

Even though I taught in the classroom for six years, I still questioned teaching my own child. I thought I was going to mess him up for life, and he was only four years old! This fear is very real for all mothers, including ones with teaching degrees, and it will consume you if you do not extinguish it as soon as possible.

The Truth: This is perhaps the most common fear of home educators yet it is the most ridiculous. Why do we believe it even for a second? God specifically choose you to be your child's parent and to teach him the most important lessons in life. Society has made us think that when our children turn five years old, we need a piece of paper saying we can teach our children. This is complete nonsense! We need to stand together and bury this fear once and for all. We should declare there is no way the enemy will use this fear against our families ever again. Your credentials do not qualify you to teach your child; your God qualifies you.

I am so passionate about this misconception that I wrote an entire book devoted to addressing this fear, *How to Teach Your Child*. If you happen to need more guidance in teaching, there are plenty of on-line resources and books available, but most importantly, you can seek guidance from the best Teacher.

God's Word: James 1:2-8- "If any of you lacks wisdom, you should ask God, who gives generously to all without finding fault, and it will be given to you."

2 Corinthians 9:8- "And God is able to bless you abundantly, so that in all things at all times, having all that you need, you will abound in every good work."

God is the best school administrator, and He will provide all that you need to help your child succeed.

I am not smart enough.

This lie usually goes hand-in-hand with the former, "I'm not qualified to teach my child." I know I am not smart enough to teach my child every subject area from kindergarten to 12th grade. I do not know everything about everything, but I know the one who does and that is all that matters.

Here's the good news. You don't need to know it all to homeschool. Did you know everything about being a parent the day you gave birth to your child? No, you didn't. You just learned about being a mother along the way. The same goes for homeschooling. Just learn and grow along the journey.

The Truth: You only need to provide your child with a supportive environment and exceptional learning tools to help him excel in education. Whether the tools are a Bible, library books, DVDs, or a boxed curriculum, look for resources that make you passionate about teaching, so your child becomes passionate about learning.

God's Word: Hebrews 13:21- "Now may the God of peace, who through the blood of the eternal covenant brought back from the dead our Lord Jesus, that great Shepherd of the sheep, equip you with everything good for doing his will, and may he work in us what is pleasing to him, through Jesus Christ, to whom be glory for ever and ever."

I can't teach the high school years.

The high school years have actually been the easiest years I have homeschooled because of all the fantastic resources available. My son completed his work independently. My role was more of a facilitator since he already had instructors on-line and through video courses.

For all those parents who have worried about teaching high school, and your child is currently in elementary school, my advice is to take it day by day. Worrying about tomorrow only robs you of today.

The Truth: Yes, you can. God does not expect you to be an expert in every subject area. There are many on-line and video courses with outstanding teachers available to help you homeschool through the upper grades.

God's Word: Matthew 6:34- "Therefore do not worry about tomorrow, for tomorrow will worry about itself. Each day has enough trouble of its own."

My child won't get into college.

God is still in control. If He wants your child to attend a particular college, nothing will stop your child from attending it. Doors will fly open regardless of test scores and transcripts because of God's divine leading. We give way too much credit to curriculum, grades, and SAT scores. God deserves the glory!

Please don't race through your homeschool journey with college being the destination. I see this happen all of the time. That seems to be the ultimate goal of our society's education plan– getting into a good college. Learning is a life-long process and certainly doesn't end after college. We are homeschooling for a much deeper purpose– to raise Godly men and women. Keep an eternal focus.

I want you to visualize Jesus standing with His

arms open wide at the end of your homeschooling path. He is the goal. Every step we take in obedience along our journey is one step closer to Him.

The Truth: It is your obedience, not your ability, that God rewards. Jehovah Jireh is your provider and will supply all of your child's needs. What you are doing has eternal rewards so keep pressing towards the goal. Keep your eyes fixed upon the prize, which is way bigger than graduation from high school or attending a good college.

God's Word: Philippians 3:14- "I press on toward the goal to win the prize for which God has called me heavenward in Christ Jesus."

2 Peter 3:18- "But grow in the grace and knowledge of our Lord and Savior Jesus Christ. To him be glory both now and forever!"

I can't balance homeschooling and my other responsibilities.

The duties of motherhood can consume us and leave us wondering how we will get it all done in one day. If we are not careful to guard our hearts and minds, we can become frustrated and even depressed. We may feel stuck with no hope. We may even feel like a failure. Isn't it interesting how we can extend grace to others but tend to be so hard on ourselves?

This is an area of my life that I have let the enemy beat me up with long enough. I can easily ignore the overflowing baskets of laundry or the sink full of dishes but I have felt like a failure when it comes to preparing meals for my family. I struggle with cooking for the first two years after having a baby. Multiply that by five children and you can see that has been a very long time. For some reason my babies tend to be fussy around dinnertime, and they have to be on my hip during those hours. They do not want anyone but mama. This limits me a lot.

I have learned to utilize my crockpot to help with this. Even though those meals are delicious, they are not always low-fat or considered to be "balanced." If I don't use the crockpot, I make something simple that I can do with one arm and a toddler on my hip. The reality is most nights I wait until my husband gets home from work, so we can tag team with the little ones and dinner. This is not what I envisioned when I began homeschooling. I pictured in my mind dinners every night like you see on Pinterest. The ugly lie popped into my mind repeatedly for years around mealtime, "You are such a bad mother. You can't even provide balanced meals for your husband and children."

The point is I would beat myself up over

something I really can't control in this season of my life. One day I will be able to spend more time in the kitchen. We all have an area we currently struggle with and want to be better at. Some areas we can control and need to create a plan to improve. But for those things we cannot control, we need to get better at letting it go.

The Truth: You are loved by your Father. You are His child. Just as we don't expect our children to be perfect, He doesn't expect you to be perfect either. Isn't that a huge relief? As long as you are trying your best, He understands. And by the way, God's grace is never just enough. His grace is always far more than enough. When you are weak, He is strong.

God's Word: 2 Corinthians 12:9- "My grace is sufficient for you, for my power is made perfect in weakness. Therefore, I will boast all the more gladly about my weaknesses, so that Christ's power may rest on me."

I really stink at homeschooling. Maybe I should quit.

Usually, this comes after, "I lost my temper and yelled at my kids. I didn't finish half of what was in my lesson plans. The house is a wreck. I royally messed up and need to throw in the towel, if only it could fit in the hamper!"

Being the Godly mother that I am, I have not always handled these situations with the maturity that you would expect. When things haven't gone the way I planned in my homeschool day, I have thrown an adult temper-tantrum. Sad, I know. Please don't try to picture a lady in her forties doing this because it's quite embarrassing. I am sure God is looking down at me with the same expression I give my children when they throw a fit for not getting their way.

The Truth: Homeschooling is without a doubt a challenge and some days it will knock you on your bottom. What you need to do is get back up and do it again. If you throw a tantrum, ask for forgiveness from your family and God and move on. God's grace provides redemption, and His compassions never fail. He's all about taking broken people and making them whole.

God's Word: Hebrews 4:16- "Let us then approach God's throne of grace with confidence, so that we may receive mercy and find grace to help us in our time of need."

Lamentations 3:22-23- "Because of the Lord's great love we are not consumed, for his compassions never fail. They are new every morning; great is your faithfulness."

Did you catch that? His mercies are new every day. Praise God!

I can't homeschool with all of these interruptions.

Most homeschool moms carry the burden of feeling like they are not doing enough. As mothers, we love our children so much and want to provide the absolute best education experience for them. When our days, months, or years do not go the way we initially thought they would, we often blame ourselves. The fact is if you are doing your best at following God's leading, you are doing more than enough.

Most of the time, life's interruptions are the lessons. Caring for a newborn, foster children, a sick relative, or an elderly parent must be viewed as teachable moments. Going on a vacation to spend quality time with relatives, serving in a ministry, or volunteering on a missionary trip are more examples of God's divine appointments. These are the most important lessons you can impress upon your child's heart. Never feel guilty that the original plans in your lesson book did not get addressed. Let go of that guilt once and for all. Welcome peace when God's plan takes over your day.

The Truth: Homeschooling is about doing life with your family, not about doing lesson plans. Reset your thinking to seize every opportunity that will make an impact in your child's life for eternity. The best lessons are found in real life.

Learn to embrace the interruptions.

God's Word: Exodus 36:5- "The people are bringing more than enough for doing the work the Lord commanded to be done."

2 Peter 1:2- "Grace and peace be yours in abundance through the knowledge of God and of Jesus our Lord."

I am so confused.

Oh, how Satan likes to throw confusion our way. It reminds me of the fireballs that are thrown to the characters in popular video games. They stun the characters and cause them to shake frantically and look puzzled. Some days I closely resemble those characters when my husband walks in from work.

It isn't a huge surprise that home educators get confused. Just visit a convention or a homeschooling website. There are so many terrific choices. To make things worse, our friends who homeschool have different opinions on curriculum and teaching styles.

If you are new to homeschooling, I need you to remember this very important word, "flexibility." Homeschool moms should be gymnasts because we have all learned how to be very flexible. Your lesson plans and curriculum choices will not always work out the way you intended but that's okay. God is teaching you how to be flexible and adjust to His plan.

The Truth: The easiest way out of this confusion is to go directly to the throne, not the phone (to ask someone's opinion of what you should do). God is in control. He's got this. He really does. Just take some time to spend with Him praying and reading His Word. He will point you in the right direction, and you will know it because you will be filled with peace in making your decision.

God's Word: 1 Corinthians 14:33 (KJV)- "For God is not the author of confusion, but of peace, as in all churches of the saints."

Chapter 5
Watch out for the comparison traps.

You will find several traps along your journey. Avoid these annoyances when possible. The enemy is extremely sneaky and his main goal is destruction. In John 10:10, Jesus tells us, "The thief comes only to steal and kill and destroy; I have come that they may have life, and have it to the full."

These traps often are set off unintentionally through the words of fellow homeschool moms. That is why we never see them coming. How clever the enemy is to use our closest supporters to tear us down! These traps are set when a mom makes a comment (often not intending any harm) then "Snap!" the comparison begins.

Traps can be like weeds.

Subtle comments can stick to you like hitchhiker weeds. Sometimes you may not even know they are on you until later. But like any weeds, they can take root and spread rapidly if you don't remove them immediately.

This trap may start with a friend saying her three-year-old is now reading when you haven't even begun to teach your three-year-old the alphabet. It can begin when a fellow home educator is discussing how her son was accepted into Harvard at 16 while your child the same age is showing no interest in attending college in the future. Maybe it starts when your ten-year-old niece who's homeschooled is playing the violin in the adult symphony when your ten-year-old just mastered "Hot Cross Buns" on his recorder.

We've all heard similar comments at some time or another. We need to remind ourselves that every child is created differently according to God's purpose.

Traps can be mirages.

Things are not always what they appear to be at first glance. For instance, you are at a homeschool meeting, and a mother speaks of all the field trips she has taken her children on within the past few months (some were even international trips). Another mother talks about the five chapter books she read aloud to her children last month (all classical and living books of course). One mother discusses how she can't find a math program that has enough manipulatives since she likes to teach all her lessons with a hands-on approach.

All you are thinking at this point is that you haven't been on one field trip in a month (unless you count the grocery store), you would be elated if you read aloud just one chapter book in a school year (without toddlers constantly interrupting), and your child hasn't used a math manipulative in years (unless you count the keyboard since it's sort of hands-on.)

Just as every child is different, every teacher instructs in a unique way. Step a little closer to see how this is just a mirage. None of those moms are doing all those approaches combined at one time. It would be impossible. Each mother chooses the approach that best fits her teaching style and her child's learning style. Avoid this comparison trap.

Traps can hurt.

Stepping into an ant pile can cause instant pain, which can linger for days. A common trap in the homeschool community is the sting of a prideful comment. Ouch! Once we begin judging how others teach and what tools they teach with, we are raising ourselves up above others and becoming prideful.

Regardless of if a mother feels the Lord leading her to use more of an unschooling approach to a very structured classical approach, it is honestly none of our business how she is educating her child as long as she is seeking the Lord's guidance. Only God knows the heart of a homeschool mom and if she is doing her best. Only God knows what each individual child needs. It is between that family and God. Only He has the master plan of education for all His creation.

There is not one way to educate. That is the beauty of homeschooling. It is personalized by the hand of God. We need to encourage, inspire, and motivate each other along this path. By focusing on what we have in common and accepting our differences, we can support one another in our journeys. Just as 1 Thessalonians 5:10-12 says, "Therefore encourage one another and build each other up."

My sister home educates her children, and she uses a very different approach and curriculum than I use. I recognize we were created uniquely for God's purpose, and we both have different strengths. I embrace our differences and never feel one way is better than another (and my master's degree is in curriculum). I trust God's plan for her family, and I encourage her to follow His leading.

The Truth: God chose you to be the mother of your child, and your child will become exactly what God created him to be. God knows your strengths and weaknesses, and He hand-picked your family members. It is His divine design.

God's Word: Romans 12:4-8- "For just as each of us has one body with many members, and these members do not all have the same function, so in Christ we, though many, form one body, and each member belongs to all the others. We have different gifts, according to the grace given to each of us. If your gift is prophesying, then prophesy in accordance with your faith; if it is serving, then serve; if it is teaching, then teach; if it is to encourage, then give encouragement; if it is giving, then give generously; if it is to lead, do it diligently; if it is to show mercy, do it cheerfully."

Watch out for the comparison traps.

Chapter 6
Avoid these temptations.

I have seen the following temptations steer too many women away from God's calling. These are much bigger than stumbling blocks, lies, and comparison traps because they are dangerous pitfalls. These pitfalls are so severe that they can keep you from following God's path and have you missing out on the blessings He has waiting for you and your family. Constantly look out for these to avoid falling into them. Common pitfalls include: wanting more time to yourself, desiring the easier path, seeking control over your finances, needing rest, and staying in your comfort zone.

If I didn't homeschool, I would have more time for me.

This often appears as a random thought and then grows quickly into a false reality. This temptation has come to me after I get out of the shower and make a mistake and look into the mirror. It goes like this, "Look at your body. Boy, you sure have let yourself go. Your husband can't possibly be attracted to you anymore."

Here's a little background for you: I've had seven pregnancies (two miscarriages with one resulting in major surgery) and my body surely shows it. I have pregnancy mask on my face that did not completely fade away, stretch marks galore, sagging skin, varicose and spider veins, thinning hair from a hormone imbalance, wrinkles on my face that tend to multiply at an exponential rate, grey hair that is popping up everywhere, and so on. It's no wonder why I sometimes feel completely insecure about my body.

Next, the thoughts in my mind start swirling. Hmmm, if I didn't homeschool, I could spend a couple of hours a day at the gym addressing this body. I could even listen to whatever I wanted to on the radio while driving to the gym. I could have time to make healthy lunches for me instead of grabbing whatever I can. I could call a girlfriend and talk on the phone uninterrupted for as long as I want. I could get a tan while reading a book. The laundry would be caught up. No more dishes piling up all day in the sink. My house would be spotless. That would be the life!

Soon it becomes all about what I want to do instead of what God wants me to do. This is where I have to immediately stop and make myself listen to the Truth. I am a mother. There is nothing else I'd rather be. I struggled with infertility for years and even miscarriages. I desperately wanted to be a mother and did not care about the effects it would have on my body. I prayed and cried and prayed some more to hold babies in my arms. There was nothing that could have brought me more joy than motherhood.

The Truth: Your temptation of "me-time" may look differently. Even though the grass may look greener on the other side, let's not forget that grass still needs to be mowed. The reality is if you choose not to homeschool in exchange for more time for yourself, there still would be work to do, including: class volunteering, homework, school projects, tests to review for, catch-up work on sick days, waiting in school pick-up lines and so on.

God's Word: Galatians 6:9- "Let us not become weary in doing good, for at the proper time we will reap a harvest if we do not give up."

This is too hard!

Homeschooling is hard. Sometimes it can be really hard, and it's a natural feeling to want to stop something that is hard. This is why God reminds us to persevere and keep running the race. Some days you may be fixed on more "me-time" and contemplating sending your children to public or private school, but on other days you are considering boarding school! Yes, you know what I am talking about. We all get them, but sometimes "those days" can turn into "those months" or even "those years."

Much of the time we think homeschooling is all about our children. We place our focus on them instead of on our Creator. When we look up, we clearly see that we are also being taught lessons in our homeschool journey, such as learning to be solely dependent on Him for: strength, guidance, courage, patience, mercy, and grace.

Too often we blame our children because they won't listen to us or focus on their lessons. But sometimes we are the ones that are broken, not our children. We must learn to die to ourselves and completely submit to His plan. This could save us years of grief and stress as well as help us avoid frustration that builds when homeschooling is not going the way we originally planned.

Dying to self is not easy. It is tough stuff. It is committing your life wholeheartedly to Him. This includes accepting any hardship this may bring. Dying to your selfish desires, your own agenda, and your ideas of perfection always begins with true humility and repentance. You may think you are almost there, and then God reveals another area to surrender to Him. It can be a long process. But once you truly surrender your life to Him, which includes your homeschool day, you will be able to enjoy your journey in a much deeper way than you have ever experienced before. We will achieve victory by completely surrendering our lives to God, not by trying harder.

It's not about us. It is all about Him and His plan for your family. When you fully accept this, you will have incredible peace in your homeschool day. Discouragement will become a thing of the past because you will realize the real Teacher has complete control even on the days it looks like your homeschool day is out of control. Just relax.

The Truth: As long as we try our best, that's all that is required. Isn't it nice to know that He will reward us on our obedience to follow Him, not how we followed through with our lesson plans and curriculum? He has the best plans, as well as the best lessons. Sometimes His plan will not align with our plans. Highlight this. Remember this. This is the key to peace in your homeschool day.

All callings from the Lord are sacred, but the calling of a homeschool mom is extraordinary. You have been chosen to fulfill that calling. You are called to serve Him by serving your family with your whole heart.

God's Word: Ephesians 6:7-8- "Serve whole-heartedly, as if you were serving the Lord, not people because you know that the Lord will reward each one for whatever good they do."

Philippians 4:13- "I can do all things through Christ who strengthens me."

I have to help provide financially for my family.

In this section, I'm referring to leaving homeschooling for a full-time job. Since I began my homeschool journey, I have worked part-time most of the years. I have worked at my church, in after-school programs, tutoring other children, and writing books. Sometimes it was out of a need to make ends meet, and other times it has been to have a little extra for homeschool classes, savings, or vacations.

What I've heard too often from the enemy is this lie, "If you go back to work full-time Tamara, your life will be less stressful. You will help alleviate the heavy burden that your husband is carrying to support your family of seven. You can pay off debts quicker. You can afford nicer things."

The enemy surely knows how I dislike debt and how I desperately would like to help my husband with the financial stresses that come with our large family. I would soon catch myself thinking, "I want to help. I really do. But I can't because I am trapped at home."

Red flag alert. I used the word "trapped." That is an obvious sign that this is a lie from the enemy. When we use the word "trapped," our instinct is to break free and run away. However, I honestly do not feel trapped. I feel blessed. I am incredibly thankful to spend everyday with my children. It is what I desire most of all. How easily we can be deceived by the enemy!

Five years ago, my family experienced financial devastation. We lost everything financially in one year, including: my husband's job, our home of seven years, our credit, three college funds, partnerships for our ministry, and both of our cars. Our loss was close to half a million dollars and much of that was money we suddenly owed due to our depreciated value in our home. (We lived in one of the economically hardest hit areas in the country.) Add to that, moving 13 hours away from our family, church, and homeschool group and becoming unexpectedly pregnant with having no reliable income to support our existing family, I sank into depression. I had hit rock bottom. I just never knew how low the bottom was until this particular trial.

Weeks before my fourth child was born, we had to move again because of the lack of money to pay rent. Then we moved again in another 7 months because my husband (who has a computer engineering degree and graduated valedictorian) could not find a job in the area. He could not even get an interview after submitting more than 300 resumes. This was VERY difficult as a mom of four children who had to keep homeschooling through it all. Friends and family sent us money to help pay for our basic bills, such as electricity and water. Talk about a humbling time. Just a year prior, we were on our way to financial freedom but how quickly everything disappeared.

I will always remember the heartbreaking feelings I endured. I wrestled with all kinds of emotions, including frustration, depression, confusion, and anger. But during this time, I saw God up close. I felt His embrace like never before. I learned how to patiently wait on God's provision and His timing. That experience transformed me and made me who I am today.

During those years, I was completely torn about continuing to homeschool, even though it was what God was calling me to do. This is why I understand if you are struggling with the idea of returning to the workplace full-time. We are mothers and we want to take care of our families. If your husband is able to provide an income, no matter the amount, you must continue what God has laid on your heart to do and care for your family at home. First, completely surrender your finances to God.

Next, seek God's wisdom on how to be resourceful with your family's income, become your husband's cheerleader, and continue to pray for provision.

It is interesting to note that most of our grandmothers did not work full-time when they had children. They sometimes had side businesses for extra income but their main focus was on raising their children and being available to help their husbands. I believe it is our current society's pressures that have us feeling like we are not pulling our own weight as mothers. The reality is motherhood is a full-time job. We may not receive a paycheck or public recognition, but mothers have the most important job ever.

If you feel led to leave homeschooling to work full-time, please seek God's guidance before you make a final decision. The enemy is a master of giving false hope. Remember to factor in all of the extra expenses, such as: after-school care, daycare for younger ones, gas to go to work, food expenses for lunches and dinners on the days you'll get home late, work clothes, school supplies, school field trips, and school uniforms. Think about who will be watching your child when he is sick, during school holidays, and over summer break. Your nights will become more rushed with homework, studying for tests, and school projects. You and your children will be spending less time together so expect the family dynamics to change.

Please know it is not my intention to make you feel guilty if God is calling you back to the workplace. Always follow His leading. Just be cautious to discern if the enemy is trying to lure you away from God's calling. I recognize everyone's circumstances vary. If you believe God wants you to continue homeschooling even though you are facing a current trial, pray for His wisdom to show you how it can be done. If there's a will, there's a way, and especially if it's God's will!

I've seen widowed mothers homeschool their children. I've seen mothers take care of their disabled husbands and homeschool their children. I've seen mothers of severely handicapped children homeschool their other children. I've seen mothers who care for their elderly parents full-time and homeschool their children. And I've seen single mothers work full-time and homeschool their children. It all can be done with God's grace.

Here is an email I recently received from a dear friend about her personal struggle. It is so empowering!

The lie I struggled with for many years would have never actually been a struggle had I understood what my true Biblical role was as a wife and a mother. Years of anger and resentment brewed within my heart, which spilled over onto our homeschool days. I had allowed society to tarnish my vision of motherhood. Let's face it; society's definition is not a very respected image. I had accepted the idea that a woman must prove her value in society by working just as hard or harder as her male counterparts to achieve certain statuses outside of the home.

I had allowed the world to define how valuable I was, by what I had to offer it in terms of career accomplishments and financial achievements. I felt worthless and trapped. What I didn't realize or understand was how God has intentional roles regarding males and females, particularly when they become husbands and wives, fathers and mothers, and the definition that I had grown to accept did not conform to His.

It was very difficult for me to relinquish my independence. However, I am no longer concerned with the alleged value that society places on me. I only care now that my role pleases God, and accommodates the needs of my family. I no longer view my family as a career obstacle, but as a promotion! In my new career, I am molding little warriors for God and raising them to utilize whatever gifts God has given them.

I know that every woman is not called to stay home, but I no longer feel less valuable because I am.

The Truth: God loves you more than you can comprehend. He wants you to learn to depend solely on Him. He knows your needs and His timing is always perfect. He has not left you. He is teaching you patience. He is training you for the future. He is asking you to stop worrying and start trusting Him.

God's Word: Philippians 4:19- "And my God will meet all your needs according to the riches of his glory in Christ Jesus."

Matthew 6:31-32- "So do not worry, saying, 'What shall we eat?' or 'What shall we drink?' or 'What shall we wear?' For the pagans run after all these things, and your heavenly Father knows that you need them."

Hebrews 13:5- "Keep your lives free from the love of money and be content with what you have, because God has said, Never will I leave you; never will I forsake you."

I'm so tired and exhausted.
I don't have what it takes.

There are some mornings I do not want to get out of bed, especially when we have a packed schedule. I know once my feet hit the floor, I won't stop until midnight. I become mentally and physically exhausted. The days, weeks, or even months can drag on and little progress can be seen. It feels like I am stuck in my homeschool path without any motivation to move forward. It is during these times, I must stop and take a break for a few days or even a few weeks to regroup and reconnect heart-to-heart with my family and my Creator.

A break may be all you need to get re-energized. Other times you may have to change your course of homeschooling even though you are still running the same race. This may be a different approach to homeschooling or even a different curriculum.

How can we expect ourselves to run a good race without ever resting or getting refreshed? Homeschooling is not a sprint but a marathon. We must pace ourselves on our journeys but also allow time for rest. Picture Jesus standing on the sidelines of your race offering you a cup of water. He wants to help refresh you. Now picture Him with His arms open wide waiting for you to fall into them and rest. Accept His grace.

The Truth: You may feel overwhelmed but your labor will not go unnoticed. It will produce immense joy. God will give you the strength to fulfill His calling, but He also expects you to take breaks along the way. It's often our own fault when we find ourselves burnt out and depleted because we don't believe we deserve a break. You deserve it! Reward yourself with rest. Whether it is a few hours, days, or even weeks, take a break when you need it. Use that time to connect with God and get revitalized for your calling.

God's Word: Matthew 11:28- "Come to me, all you who are weary and burdened, and I will give you rest."

Jeremiah 31:25- "I will refresh the weary and satisfy the faint."

I feel God is calling me to homeschool but...

I'm pretty sure God has heard every excuse before. If God is calling you, He will give you more than you need to get the job done, but this will require obedience from you and obedience is often costly. It may cost you more time on your knees seeking His direction, or it may cost you some personal sacrifices.

When I was called into ministry seven years ago, I thought all God wanted me to do was write a book for my small homeschool group. Later, the book was printed to share with a larger audience. Next, He called me to speaking. Who me? God certainly had the wrong person this time. The lines of communication must have been crossed somewhere. I did not like people staring at me- at all!

I had two choices- obey God and step out of my comfort zone or disobey God and stay where I was comfortable. My speaking opportunities turned into radio interviews and then into television interviews. I laugh when people tell me I am a natural on television. If they only knew; I never sleep more than a couple of hours the night before, I always feel nauseous on the drive to the studio, and I have an ongoing stomachache until the shoot is over.

I am still in awe of how God is constantly stretching me. It is sometimes a painful process, believe me, but I have seen such growth in ways I could have never imagined. The feedback I have received from others has become my encouragement to continue. Every book review, email, and card is treasured. In fact, I have every comment and review printed off and saved in a journal. Those kind words are dear to my heart and serve as a great reminder of staying the course.

I share this story with you because God did not call the most equipped person. There are professional writers and broadcasters who write and speak much better than I can, but for some reason, He called me to encourage parents. It is still hard for me to step out in faith and follow Him, but there is no better place to be than in the center of God's will.

Another point I'd like to mention about obedience is delayed obedience *is* disobedience. Think of when you ask your child to do something, and he finds an excuse not to do it or he says he'll do it later. It may frustrate you that he is not listening to your directions. It may also anger you if your child asks, "Why?"

This is how God feels when we make excuses and do not respond immediately to His directions or when we question Him. I can hear God saying the same response to me as I tell my children, "Because I said so, that's why. That's all you need to know."

The Truth: Faith and obedience go hand in hand. If you do not have faith in God's plan and obey Him, you will miss out on some of the most exciting experiences of your life. You cannot stay where you are and go with God. You cannot continue doing things your way and accomplish God's purposes His way. For you to do the will of God, you must adjust your life to Him, His purposes, and His ways. The will of God will never take you where the grace of God will not protect you.

God's Word: Romans 8:28- "And we know that in all things God works for the good of those who love him, who have been called according to his purpose."

Proverbs 16:3- "Commit to the Lord whatever you do, and he will establish your plans."

Ephesians 3:20- "Now to him who is able to do immeasurably more than all we ask or imagine, according to his power that is at work within us."

Avoid these temptations.

Chapter 7
Fruit of the Spirit

The fruit of the Spirit is something only the Holy Spirit can produce in the life of a believer. As we live a life of obedience and faithfulness, that fruit grows and develops in our lives. If we live by the Spirit, we shall see fruit in our present circumstances, and we'll also have a rich reward waiting for us in heaven. That is such reassuring news!

I encourage you to study the fruit of the Spirit and learn how they can transform your school day. These are fruit every homeschool mom desperately needs. In Galatians 5:22, we learn "The fruit of the Spirit is love, joy, peace, patience, kindness, goodness, faithfulness, gentleness and self-control."

This powerful verse can renew your mind, heart, and ability to be all that God has intended you to be. For a radio program that discusses how each fruit impacts your parenting and teaching, visit my site and take the 7 week challenge- *www.tinyurl.com/7weekchallenge*

Colossians 1:6- "The gospel is bearing fruit and growing throughout the whole world– just as it has been doing among you since the day you heard it and truly understood God's grace."

Chapter 8
Your journey continues.

It is my hope that you have seen how much you are loved by your Father, so you can accept His abundant provision of grace. Accept the grace to make mistakes. Accept the grace to take a nap when you are exhausted. Accept the grace to not feel guilty any longer. Accept the grace to live with dignity in the present and with hope in the future.

I have enjoyed learning alongside of you while our heavenly Father led the way, but now it is time for our paths to part. How reassuring it is to know we are never alone as we continue on our separate paths. Jesus is always by your side ready to gently take your hand and lead the way. Stay the course. Keep your eyes fixed on Him. No longer be deceived by hiding God's Truth in your heart.

You are a courageous and faithful woman of God. You are loved by the King. You are His daughter. Until we meet again, may you accept His abundant grace and peace as you continue your homeschool journey.

You are invited to visit me anytime for encouragement and creative teaching tips at *www.teachingwithtlc.com*. I have lots of videos, resources, and creative teaching tips that you may enjoy.

Please take a minute to write a sentence or two wherever you purchased this book to let me know how you liked it. Whenever I hear back from my readers through a review, it is like opening a present. I get so excited!

For a document to print and use as a reminder of the topics discussed in this book, visit *www.tinyurl.com/graceforyou*

Grace For the Homeschool Mom *By: Tamara L. Chilver*

The Lie	The Truth	God's Reassuring Grace
~I Don't Have the Courage You Do	courageous. You were created to be the leader for your child.	Be strong and courageous. Do not be afraid or terrified because of them, for the Lord your God goes with you; he will never leave you nor forsake you. 2 Timothy 2:1 Be strong in the Grace that is in Christ Jesus.
~I Don't Have Time To Homeschool Like You Do	Homeschooling may not be God's will for every family, but we still need to seek His wisdom and gain a clear understanding of His purpose in this area of our lives and adjust our plans and schedule accordingly.	Proverbs 19:21 Many are the plans in a person's heart, but it is the Lord's purpose that prevails. Psalm 90:12 Teach us to number our days, that we may gain a heart of wisdom
~Aren't You Worried Your Child May Not Be Socialized?	Other children are inside four walls all day while your child has been to the grocery store, the bank, and the park. Remember, the definition of socialization is to know how to act appropriately in various situations.	Romans 12:2 Do not conform to the pattern of this world, but be transformed by the renewing of your mind. Then you will be able to test and approve what God's will is—his good, pleasing and perfect will.
The Lie	The Truth	God's Reassuring Grace
~I Am the Worst Example of a Homeschool Mom	None of us are perfect. We will make mistakes no matter how hard we try not to, this includes our children. The great news is God already knew every detail about you and your child when He called you to homeschool. Be confident in your calling. He is working on you and through you.	Matthew 5:11-12 Blessed are you when people insult you, persecute you and falsely say all kinds of evil against you because of me. Rejoice and be glad, because great is your reward in heaven.

About the Author

Tamara L. Chilver is a popular homeschool author and an influential blogger who is passionate about providing parents with fun and creative teaching tips. Tamara's bachelor's degree is in elementary education, and her master's degree is in elementary curriculum. Before entering the homeschooling world 16 years ago with her five children, Tamara was a public school elementary teacher, a private school curriculum coordinator, and a private tutor. Tamara uses her diverse background in education to empower parents with confidence while simplifying learning methods. She is currently a speaker, television contributor and a best-selling author.

Additional Resources

How to Teach Your Child addresses one of the most common concerns homeschool moms have– How do I teach my child? Tamara L. Chilver reveals the tools of the trade while providing parents with simple teaching tips in the core subject areas that actively engage children in the learning process.

In this practical guide, you will learn how to:

- Make learning FUN.
- Enhance your existing curriculum.
- Use successful teaching tips.
- Prevent burnout for you and your child.
- Save money by using practical teaching tips.

In **Simplify Your Homeschool Day**, you will learn:

•Practical tips that can save you hours of teaching, planning, and grading each week;
•Effective communication techniques that can eliminate frustration and dramatically impact your child's learning;
•When you should enlist help;
•Creative learning strategies that can be applied on the go; and
•How to pursue your own passions.

These time-saving tips will increase your child's enjoyment of learning by reducing the time it takes him to complete school work without decreased learning. Put some extra time back into your day right away!

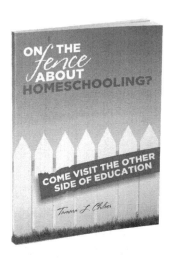

Do you find yourself sitting on the fence between traditional education options and homeschooling? Are you sensing God might be calling you over to home-school? Is fear keeping you from exploring your options?

Let Tamara Chilver gently guide you through the homeschool world in *On the Fence About Homeschooling?* As a former school teacher and now a veteran homeschool educator, she shares her personal journey with you while giving you the benefits, along with the sacrifices of homeschooling. After reading this book, you will be able to more confidently make a decision concerning the path that is best for your family.

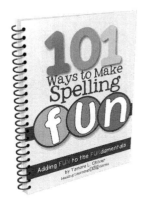 

Transform your child's spelling and writing lessons with these creative tips in *101 Ways to Make Spelling Fun* and *101 Ways to Make Writing Fun*. Why make learning fun? Research consistently shows that children learn more when they are actively engaged in the learning process and having fun.

Created for preschoolers up to sixth graders these engaging activities can be used as a stand-alone or as a compliment to any curriculum. There are activities that address all types of learning styles. These modern and lively writing and spelling assignments cross into many subject areas, including: reading, writing, math, music, government, and art. But let's not forget that these activities are just plain fun!

www.homeschooltshirt.com

20922013R00048

Made in the USA
San Bernardino, CA
29 April 2015